2016 Li'

RUN.
JOURNEY.
BECOME

The 3100-mile footrace
of a lifetime

Stutisheel Lebedev

Run. Journey. Become
The 3100-mile footrace of a lifetime
By Stutisheel Oleg Lebedev

The author is the first runner from the former Soviet countries to complete the world's longest certified footrace of 3100 miles. In this book, he shares his personal experiences and discoveries and the inspiration of achieving incredibly challenging goals. For an ultra race such as this, you cannot solely depend on the common sense of daily life. The greater the distance and running time, the more you need to look for the support from within, to use unconventional solutions and rely on intuition and inner feelings.

If you are not aware of what you can do, this is the book for you. For your victories over the limitations, fear and impossibility. For your inspiration in becoming a true human being.

Design and layout: Dewos Team
Pictures: Utpal Marshall, Jowan, Alakananda

Front cover - Stutisheel's last lap at the 3100-Mile Race with the Race flag, 2015.

Back cover - Stutisheel's ninth finish at the 3100-Mile Race, 2015.

For additional information please visit
www.Stutisheel.org

ISBN-13: 978-1530888184
ISBN-10: 1530888182

Words of Appreciation

Publication of this book was made possible due to
special contributions from

Kedar Misani and **Prachar Stagemann**.

Special thanks for the dedicated support of

*Nripal Petersen, Bhashwar Hart, Adhirata Keefe,
Artem Polozhii and Lunthita Duthely.*

Brief Overview

The annual Self-Transcendence 3100-Mile Race was called "The Mount Everest of ultra marathons" by The New York Times. This is the longest certified footrace in the world. Athletes are able to test themselves in a format unlike any other ultra-marathon event. They must average 59.6 miles per day - for 52 straight days - in order to reach 3100 miles. The surface is concrete sidewalks around a playground, ball fields, and the confines of a vocational high school, and all in a city neighbourhood setting. They must run these miles in an 18-hour daily format.

The physical and psychological demands are prodigious, if not overwhelming. Thus, participation is limited to invited athletes who have a resume of multi-day running experience and elite endurance abilities. Usually it's a field of up to 14 runners.

The race was founded in 1997 by Sri Chinmoy (1931-2007) - athlete, philosopher, composer, artist, spiritual leader and peace visionary.

He said,

If we really want to go onward,
And fly upward and dive inward -
There is nothing
That can actually resist us.[1]

Currently there are 38 runners from 18 countries who have been able to cross the finish line of the 3100-Mile Race during its 19 editions.

In 2004, Stutisheel Lebedev from Kyiv became the first runner from the former Soviet countries to finish the Race. At present he is #16 in overall ranking and #3 by the number of finishes - 9.

Table of Contents

Foreword

*A journey of a thousand miles begins with
a single step.*

Confucius

When I started to write a book "How I spent the summer of 2015," I felt that as soon as I tried to put the experience of the 3100-Mile Race into words, I had immediately separated it from reality. The written expression was merely a truncated view, a faint resemblance of the original.

I can only imagine what impossibility spiritual Masters are facing, when they see the Truth in all its radiance, greatness and immensity ... and then try to express their vision and experience through the various means that are available to human beings. It's like trying to put the ocean in a nutshell. But if the music, books and other expressions of the Truth are so inspiring, what can we say about the Original Itself?

It seems that the only way to get full and undistorted

experience is to become the experience itself, to become the Truth.

When Arpan DeAngelo first started the Race back in 2004, he said: "By helping runners of the 3100-Mile Race all these years, countless times coming to the track, I thought I knew almost everything about the 3100-Mile. But when I started, I realized that I knew nothing! The only way to comprehend the distance is to start it."

So, this is the strategic direction for those who want to have a real experience of the longest footrace in the world - the Self-Transcendence 3100-Mile Race. However, I'll try my best to convey my own experiences, my tears and smiles, my ups and downs. To a certain extent, my video reports that I did on a daily basis complemented the picture of the Race. These can be viewed at Vimeo - https://vimeo.com/user4566270.

In addition, those who want to be in tune with the latest news and discoveries of the Race are welcome to subscribe to my newsletter at *www.Stutisheel.org*

As always, the inspiration for a new book and its insight came during the 3100-Mile Race itself. With that, let us begin:

Run. Journey. Become
The 3100-mile footrace of a lifetime

Stutisheel
New York, 2016

Discipline-Power

If one can stick to the training throughout the many long years, then will power is no longer a problem. It's raining? That doesn't matter. I'm tired? That's beside the point. It's simply that I just have to.

Emil Zatopek

I love running workouts – training in preparation for any competition. My experience tells me that when an important race is scheduled, then discipline, concentration, willpower and a lot of other good qualities will come to help you use the precious months prior to reaching the starting line in the most productive way. This is my advice to all rookies: if you want to make serious progress, sign up for the competition and start a regular training program. Just running for fun definitely does not bring the same unprecedented progress as proper training.

During the winter of 2015, I had the perfect conditions to prepare for my 11th start in the 3100-Mile Race: I trained in Florida, where the summer never ends. Through almost every training session, I had a wonderful, positive drive and felt the fullness of life in all its beauty. Again and again, I return to the formula: the fullness of life lies in motion. When I run, swim or bike I feel tremendously better. Inspiration-waves come and the world around me becomes beautiful and awesome.

In January and February I was "resting" – running and biking a total of about 30 miles per week. At the beginning of March, I started to increase my training volume. Twenty-mile workouts were added to my schedule, bringing me to 60-75 miles per week. In April, I ran a milestone marathon - 26.2 miles in 3:31. After that I went on a 10-day Madal Bal cleansing diet. During the diet I was not training hard because toxins are most effectively eliminated when a person is in a relaxed state. This was the only time when I could have adhered to that diet without major damage to my training. I still had the most intense workout schedule for the month of May ahead of me.

On my birthday in May, I ran a traditional 50 km during the training in New York City. At the end of the workout, I recorded my feelings.

When I run I feel a true fulness of life. I recall Sri Chinmoy's dedication to runners of the 3100-Mile Race: "I am the

world's longest distance daring and shattering runner."
When I'm on the move, I grow into it...

In May, my goal was to run a lot and recover quickly. I ran six days a week, including one speed workout. I was now entering the peak of my training:

> Wed - 17 km, pace 6:07 min/km
> Thu - 10 km, speed-ups, pace of 4 min/km
> Fri - 24 km, pace 6:02 min/km
> Sat - 70 km, pace 6:19 min/km, average heart rate 123 bpm (+ 33C, 80% humidity)
> Sun - 45 km relaxed, pace 6:32 min/km
> Mon - 11 km, pace 6:13 min/km
> Tue - rest

In total I ran 710 km (440 miles) during this last intense training month. For three weeks I went beyond 160 km (100 miles).

Summer came a month earlier than usual in Florida. After one long race, when I hit the heat wall of +34C, I had to use a range of measures to help the body cope with the extreme conditions of high heat and 80% humidity. I call it "anti-heat pill." (I will talk about this a little later.) In general, although the conditions were extreme, they perfectly reproduced the New York combat conditions of our 3100-Mile Race. This adverse situation was really to my benefit.

May 2015

	Monday	Tuesday	Wednesday	Thursday	Friday	Saturday	Sunday	Weekly Totals
	27 Jamaica Running – 11.78 km 1:10:51	28 Flushing Running – 15.41 km 1:33:56	29	30 Jamaica Running – 17.43 km 1:42:15	1 Jamaica Running – 24.00 km 2:16:20	2 2 mile race – 3.24 km 0:12:29	3 Cunningham Park – 30.46 km 3:00:24	Distance 102.32 km Time 9:56:17 Calories 7,374 C
	4 Birthday 50K Run, New York – 50.09 km 4:57:22	5 Cunningham Park Running – 11.31 km 1:11:46	6 Clearwater Beach Open Water Swimming – 0.26 km 0:11:58	7 Safety Harbor Running – 24.01 km 2:22:29	8 Safety Harbor Speed-Ups – 8.23 km 0:46:22	9 35 km; Safety Harbor Running – 35.39 km 3:28:23	10 Run 55K; Safety Harbor Running – 40.34 km 4:01:34	Distance 169.63 km Time 16:59:55 Calories 10,860 C
	11 Safety Harbor Running – 11.31 km 1:08:35	12	13 Run 24K; Safety Harbor Running – 24.05 km 2:25:17	14 Workout 8*200; speed ups – 11.63 km 1:08:40	15 Running 17K; Safety Harbor Running – 17.50 km 1:45:53	16 Safety Harbor Running – 41.29 km 4:08:41	17 55K – 55.02 km 5:56:59	Distance 160.79 km Time 16:34:06 Calories 12,184 C
	18 Safety Harbor Running – 12.03 km 1:18:07	19	20 Run 24K; Safety Harbor Running – 17.62 km 1:47:41	21 Run 8K + speedups; speed-ups 3*1km – 9.63 km 0:53:53	22 Running 17K; Safety Harbor Running – 24.05 km 2:24:58	23 70K – longest training 2015 – 70.03 km 7:22:18	24 45K easy – 45.70 km 4:58:26	Distance 179.06 km Time 18:45:22 Calories 7,624 C
	25 Safety Harbor Running – 11.09 km 1:09:01; Tubing/Swimming Rainbow River – 2.62 km 1:30:01	26	27 Run 24K; Safety Harbor Running – 24.08 km 2:22:26	28 Workout 8*200; speedups – 9.62 km 0:54:47	29 Running 17K; Safety Harbor Running – 17.53 km 1:45:52	30 35 km; Safety Harbor Running – 46.01 km 4:43:08	31 32K easy – 32.40 km 3:28:33	Distance 143.34 km Time 15:53:46 Calories 9,067 C

Month Totals: All Activities | Activities: 29 | Distance: 710.53 km | Time: 73:42:23 | Calories: 43,884 C

Week | Month | Year | Weekly Totals | Today

A full actual training workouts from Garmin sport watches.

That was the outer aspect of my training. I had a good luck with the inner part, too. I was at meditation practice in Bali in February. Then in New York in April - when the anniversary of Sri Chinmoy's arrival in the West was being celebrated. Everything nicely fit my holistic preparation plan for the start of that year's 3100-Mile Race.

I did my homework, you could say. What will happen at the Race itself, no one can ever predict. In that regard, this Race is particularly interesting. Participants must be ready for anything. From the outer point of view, we did not have even one year of ideal conditions: one year, asphalt was being laid; another year, concrete sidewalks were being repaired, and still another time, artificial turf was being installed at the adjacent sport field.

Even now, there are scaffoldings at the college around which we run. Reconstruction will last most of the summer, and this means dust, noise, heavy vehicles. Nevertheless, the scaffolding provides one advantage in this urban multi-day race (as it is called by the race director Rupantar): protection from the sun and the rain.

Your Own Style

If you're afraid - don't do it.
If you're doing it - don't be afraid!

Genghis Khan

My wife Atandra and I arrived in New York two weeks prior to the start of the 3100-Mile Race, which was scheduled for June 14. We received a surprise "culture shock" from the city. During the winter months in Florida, we were accustomed to a mild climate and gentle people. New York greeted us with rain, cold, and nervous energy. Unfortunately, the city's "nervous" atmosphere was quite tangible at the beginning of the 3100-Mile Race. Our first few weeks were jittery and unsettled: the weather was jumping back and forth between cold to hot, and the repair of the Thomas Edison High School was in its zenith. Then another repair of the college across the street started influencing our balance.

I also failed to establish an even run with my own

style. Ashprihanal, Galya and Atmavir set an incredible pace: in the first day, Ashprihanal ran 94 miles and then 83 and 79 jn the following two days. Galya racked up 86, 76 and 73 miles. Atmavir ran in third place with 82, 72 and 77 miles. Even 70 miles per day seemed to be insufficient for the race. I felt that I was well prepared; maybe I was. But I could not get a grip on doing at least 70 miles per day.

At the second, fourth, twelfth and then seventeenth days, I experienced a sort of breakdown and was reduced to walking. Partially because of my desire to achieve a decent level of daily miles in the beginning of the race, I broke down my reserve forces. As always, the wisdom and the right thoughts come later, when writing a memoir. Now I can say for sure that if I had not chased big miles, tried to take root in my own style and did not "sag" in the transition period, I would have saved a lot of nervous energy, and ultimately even reduced my run by a few days.

But there was something else. After the finish, running once around the 3100 loop, I suddenly thought that my rejection of the city had worked against me: that was bad, that was wrong.

Sri Chinmoy pointed out a few times that for a good start in a big event, it's vital to arrive at least three days before the starting date to establish good relations with the soul of the city and the country. In this way, the city will befriend you and provide internal support. It seemed that was exactly what I had failed to do in the

**Receiving blessing-support from Sri Chinmoy
at the 3100-Mile Race in 2004.**

beginning. Finally, in the second half of the race, I began to feel the atmosphere of the "good old 3100," when Sri Chinmoy was coming to the track: the high states, support from the track itself, the flow of energy that brought an inner thrill....

One of the most common question at my lectures and meetings is what sport shoes I'm running in. The choice of shoes, as well as sports nutrition, which I will discuss later, is vital and unique. One of the main characteristics of the 3100-Mile distance is that it is extremely long. One of the journalists estimated that it takes about 10 million steps for an athlete to complete it. And during these millions of steps, even the slightest problem in the shoe can pop up that would not appear in shorter distances: for example, the height of the heel lift, tongue discomfort, the width of the shoes and other things.

There are a few general directions that need to be taken into account during the initial choice of sport shoes. But ultimately, practice is the final judge.

For example, for most of the runners, and I'm one of them, the heel placement slopes to the side, thus causing bending and torsion of the shoe. This is called pronation. After months of training, the heels wear out and the shoes are warped. Some brands put small weights on the other side of the sole to level the "rolling." It is interesting that in the 3100-Mile Race, our shoes wear out in three or four days! The shoe heel is worn down, the shoes become skewed, and the Achilles tendons immediately feel it. Despite my best intentions to save my shoes and not have to invest money in multiple pairs, it takes me an average of 16 pairs to complete the 3100-Mile Race.

In long races on hard surfaces, the cushioning is very important. They say that the running shoes need to be "soft." But the disadvantage in wearing soft sneakers is a loss of stability. As always, we need a golden balance.

Throughout my running career, which spans more than thirty years, I have tried different brands. It happened that in 1994, when I became interested in long distances and ran my first marathon, I naturally came to Asics. And all my PBs – in the marathon, the 47-mile race and world's longest 3100-Mile Race – I set in sneakers of that brand.

16 pairs of shoes awaiting the start in 2015.
No pair will be left unworn...

Asics provide cushioning in form of the gel under the heel, and in some models under the toe. This is the real salvation for running on hard surfaces.

The remaining points of the selection process of a particular model depend on individual taste and properties of the foot. I repeat - it is strictly individual. If you are serious about it, you have to find a store with a treadmill and a good specialist who can describe weak areas in your running style and address the various models for the solution. The rest - only practice can verify.

Sometimes I experiment with shoes following strong advice of my 3100 friends, who run in a variety of brands. It's amazing how little things, such as exces-

"Light" modification of the sport shoes.

sive foot rise, firmer cushioning or a very soft, light but unstable sole - always brought me back to the verified Asics brand.

Usually I train in the more expensive sneakers of that brand, but for the Race itself I'm looking for a compromise between price and quality, because I need 16 pairs of brand new running shoes for each 3100-Mile Race. Eleven years ago, I used a model of the Asics Gel 1100 series. Now the series has taken a new birth under the name Asics GT 1000. I'm buying running shoes 1.5 sizes larger than my usual ones with the maximum width - 4E. After four to six days of running, my feet become flattened and markedly bigger.

I cut off the top of the shoes immediately to avoid the slightest rubbing of toes and to increase ventilation. Other runners are cutting out parts that can provoke injuries and rub sores: sides and heel tabs. The running shoe producers would probably be horrified if they saw these "modifications" of their products. But that's life: it's much easier to buy new shoes than to make new feet or legs.

What models do other runners prefer? Ashprihanal ran in Adidas Energy Boost last race and was very pleased. Galya runs mainly in Mizuno Inspire 10, but he loves probably the widest variety of brands. Pranjal prefers Asics Nimbus. You can see a complete diversity because everybody has his/her own foot placement and running style.

Enjoying Every Moment

In the middle of difficulty lies opportunity.

Albert Einstein

As you probably know, the 3100-Mile Race has its transition period. And unlike in other races, this can be quite lengthy – 10 days or even two weeks. During this time, we watch how the body adapts to the daily rhythm of heavy loads. At first, the feet are quite sensitive to the inconvenience of shoes, hard concrete surface, thousand of similar steps.

Also, the body tries to get rid of everything unnecessary, things that prevents effective digestion. The stomach is also actively responding to food it does not like. It's at the beginning of the Race that many runners have visible redness on the feet; this is one way that the body eliminates chemicals and wastes. The skin is still quite sensitive to constant, even extreme exposure to the sun. In general, during the transition period, you often feel quite unwell or even sick. We accept this calmly; it will pass anyway. As Winston Churchill said, "If you're going through hell, keep going."

But still, it would be nice to invent some mechanism to skip the transition period, to go directly to where you are already fully functional, energy is flowing and everything is super positive. But no ... we are compelled to enjoy every moment. As in life, ups and downs, waves of inspiration and disappointing events, are intertwined. We must learn to allocate the most importance to vital things that will support us at all times and to see the positive side, which definitely exists in everything.

**12 self-giving runners at the start
of the 2015 3100-Mile Race.**

Adamantine Determination

To have determination
Is to be halfway
To the goal.

Sri Chinmoy[2]

On the one hand, I always want to run in the flow, spontaneously, without tension. On the other hand, this spontaneity and acceptance of everything that comes without proper determination turns into just following the current. You can be picked up by other currents that might provoke a great disaster. Somehow, if you do not resist difficult days, they will significantly slow you down and perhaps invite other difficult and slow days into your life. Yet, you must have an adamantine determination to move forward at maximum speed.

After several days of walking, when I had exhausted all the spare time reserve, I realized that one more day of walking would prevent me from meeting the deadline of 52 days. This happened after I had covered only half the distance.

Somehow I concentrated, pulled forward my determination and no longer allowed walking days to come near me. I finished with18 excellent days. Of course, many factors affected it - inner concentration, the special flow of Grace from Above, the presence and great support of our super doctor Kausal Cortella for the last ten days of the race... Still, my experience tells me that it is exactly through determination that Grace and Energy from Above work most effectively.

**Last day of the 2014 Race -
on the way to my Personal Best.**

Inner Cry

He who conquers others is strong.
He who conquers himself is mighty.

Lao Tzu

Everything that is connected with long races requires a certain attitude when your plans go wrong. I think the Supreme just cracks up when we build our long-term plans and say that this is the only way to achieve happiness.

In 2012 I had the most dramatic event in my entire history of ultra-running. I got a shin splint on the 36th day, which in itself is unusual to the extreme. Runners are going through that kind of injuries at the beginning of the race. But to get it at the second half of the 3100-Mile Race is a huge exception from the rule. Later I felt that there was some inner reason for that. Anyway, after five days of walking slowly, I got up to the level of 120 laps per day. I came to the final stretch with full hope of meeting the deadline. And then - the full moon! It compelled me to walk again, and all my plans to finish in 52 days simply vanished.

After that, something even worse happened: I lost all motivation. Nothing could encourage me to run. I was walking, eating, sleeping, killing time ... It was just awful. This is the test not for the weak, who - when plans go wrong – feel totally lost. Again, when properly absorbed, such a situation could be a powerful experience that provides an imminent takeoff. Here, we need flexibility and determination at the same time – plus reliance and trust in the Author of the True Plans of your life.

Through many years of races and repeated changes of plan A, I see that the most important thing is your aspiration to do everything that you can at the moment and not to be discouraged. Thus the term "determined surrender" was born. You take whatever twists of fate you are given, do not give up and try to do the maximum with your capacities.

In such difficult moments, I often recall the words of Sri Chinmoy:

> *Our real failure takes place*
> *When we give up making*
> *Further attempts.*[3]

On a lighter note: "Every boxer knows what happens when you put down your hands."

I had a few difficult days during the 2015 Race, when I felt like a tiny, helpless grain of sand in the vast universe of God. That grain of sand was subject to all the influences of the sun, the moon, various elemental forces ... It seemed that nothing of my past experiences and outer knowledge could ease my fate.

On the thirty-first day, I walked the minimal number of laps during the Race – 51 – a total of 27 miles. This was perhaps the worst day of the Race for me. But I'm still grateful for this experience because it allowed me to see my real self. Here is what I recorded in a report that day:

"Everyone has their own weaknesses. Nobody has a perfect body, whatever you do. My running happening in waves. Until the next "blackout" as I call it. Sometimes running set lasts for 10-15 days, sometimes blackout happening every other day ...

To rely on your body's strength is simply impossible - it does not work. Same with the power of your vital, strength of thoughts, intellect. Everything fails you. And it fails you in the most critical moment, as it turns out.

What remains? Something deeper. That even in a state where there are no forces at all moves you forward - your inner cry. I can only smile... it's still in me.

What is surprising is that despite all the outer things that are trying to drop you below ground zero, there is an inner strength, some higher power that is trying to raise you. I am more than confident that tomorrow I'll run, and tomorrow it will be a different story."

Follow Your Heart

*Follow your way and let people say
anything they want.*

Dante Alighieri

One of the main questions the runners of the
3100-Miles Race are asked, especially those
who participate more than once: Why do you
even go out to the starting line? In fact, the whole race
is a complete negation of common sense. We do not
receive valuable prizes for finishing the Race; we gain
no worldwide fame or other outer honours. Quite often
my participation in the Race meant the risk of dismissal
from work (and it often worked out that I lost my job).
Each runner is investing thousands of dollars in order
to be subjected to the most severe test of their body, of
their entire being. Yet, many come to the start again and
again. I belong to this club.

I can say for sure what motivation is not at work
here:

- the desire to become famous
- the need to prove something to others or even to yourself

In my experience, all the external motivations are extremely traumatic. Here everything is less dependent even on distance. You can be badly injured even in a 100m race and spend a long time recovering. But in the 3100-Mile Race, all artificial motivations disappear after about three days of running. If you do not find deeper inspiration to continue, there is no chance you will be able to finish the Race.

Below is the quote from Boiragi's song "He's a Runner":

If you ask him, what he is doing it for? He might just look at you and say: "I'm not really sure." But he knows deep in his heart that the role's been cast and he has to play his part.

I have a complete feeling that this is my role: to be a runner of the 3100-Mile Race. I do not compete with anyone. I just try to do my best. Of course, other runners inspire me, and I can follow someone to do my own high mileage. But overall, I put a mark for my performance myself - whether I did everything I could. Of course, everything does not always go smoothly. But that's the charm! As in the joke: Everything goes according to plan. Just plan is poor.

That's our goal - to learn to accept any plan and

make the most of every situation. I think this is, first of all, the safest approach, devoid of the large risk of injuries. And second - it is very joyful. Plus, it works!

One day I got a mischievous idea to formulate the signs of the world's longest distance runner.

You are a 3100-Mile runner if:

- To the morning question: "How do you feel?", you answer "I will start to run, and it will become clear."

- During one lap you can cradle just one thought in your head, which often does not survive to the end of the lap.

- You learn to communicate in short sentences, in which the whole meaning of life can be expressed.

- You eat about 50 times a day and still lose weight.

- The greatest encouragement for you is: "You're looking good today!"

- In the morning you start to dream about a 15-minute break that is another seven hours ahead.

- You go to bed at 1 a.m. or 2 a.m., or even later, only to get up at 5 a.m. and head out for a morning jog, which goes on for 18 hours.

- Your legs cannot run, and your mind cannot speak.

- You wear out 15 pairs of shoes in 50 days.

- You believe that all injuries and crises can be cured by running.

- Instead of going on a wonderful vacation, you invest several thousand of dollars to run on a concrete half-mile loop in one of the most unsightly districts of the New York.

- You are a true 3100-Mile runner if you go against all common sense and come back to repeat the race because you follow your heart.

This inner call is expressing itself powerfully and brightly, especially in life of the top 3100-Mile runners. I remember a story about Madhupran when, after his not-so-successful Race in 2004, he had a dream with Sri Chinmoy, who encouraged him to start again. Madhupran shared the dream with his wife. And she, remembering the last hard race, was a little scared and said that he could go back not as a runner, but as helper. Madhupran then replied very firmly: "I am a runner!" He returned in 2006, only to set a new world record.

After Ashprihanal's finish this year, when he surpassed Madhupran's nine-year-old record by almost 24 hours, I heard a story about him. On the verge of the race, he dreamed that Sri Chinmoy asked him to set a new record.

In the dream, Ashprihanal said: "But Guru, I do not have the capacity."

Guru replied: "I'll give you the capacity!"

Galya Balatskyy had a few big problems that could easily cancel his start: a knee injury – a meniscus tear that had developed a year earlier, plus inflamed teeth. There is a very subtle line between common sense and fanaticism. At any rate, he started the 3100-Mile Race, feeling assurance from Above, and set an almost unsurpassable record. But that is not the main point. According to him, he received a very strong positive experience from that Run - a sacred gift in life.

When you come close to your body's limits - it is always on the verge of the injury. But if there is enough receptivity, Grace from Above performs miracles. I've seen it in my life and in the lives of my friends.

Galya Balatskyy (right) and Ashprihanal Aalto enjoy walking the hill.

Best Friends

A true friend is a miracle performed by God Himself.

Sri Chinmoy[4]

The first time I heard this statement was from Ashprihanal: all of my best friends - at the 3100-Mile Race. Over time it became true for me, too. And it's not about individuals who have their ups and downs in everyday life. This is a special state that exists during the Race.

When you are going through all the challenges together with other runners, you can see their aspiration, determination, willpower and also their oneness and empathy. Somehow it all brings us closer to each other with a special bond. All the masks and artificial layers fall down very quickly. I am in awe of these true people who emerge. Interestingly, during the Race we can come very close with somebody, running hundreds of miles together. But after the finish, when the maya of life covers us again, we go away to our separate lives.

In fact, only during the race do I experience such intense feelings of joy and pride for the achievements of my friends or concerns and desire to help when problems occur. We are involved much less with our 3100-Mile friends in everyday life. But still I cherish the idea that if you lack real friends, they certainly can be found at the 3100-Mile Race.

With Galya - better together.

Once I read that the Supreme Himself creates the connection between real friends. Everyone has some different and unique quality that he/she responds to. In my case, when I see reliability, and sincere care for progress of others - no matter what you possess and who you are - something definitely responds in my heart. Such selfless support touches me the most, and I try to express it to other people, too.

I have real friends not only among the runners. All those who are somehow attracted to the 3100-Mile exhibit their best qualities.

This year I was once again amazed by doctor Kausal Cortella, who came from Italy for 10 days near the end of the race to "fix" us. He was happier than we were when he was able to find an effective solution to increase our running speed. Absolutely sincere, selfless support! I must say that he is a professional of the highest level: an Ayurvedic doctor, homeopath, specialist on subtle energies. And he is constantly learning. His knowledge and skills are amazing! Plus, he broke away from his busy schedule, sacrificing his trip to the August Celebrations to help us complete the longest race in the world.

The fullness of life
Lies in dreaming
And manifesting
The impossible dreams.

Mission accomplished: With Kausal Cortella
before his flight home.

In 2009 during one brief visit to him when I had a breakdown, he predicted that in 10 days I would achieve my full potential at the Race. And then "God alone knows what will happen!" That year I set a personal best of 48 days and 12 hours, which I was able to transcend only five years later. At the same time, working on my chronically weak kidneys and liver in the second half of the race, he made an interesting discovery. This chronic hereditary weakness in the kidneys began to develop in my childhood, triggered by a heavy emotional experience. We have heard the saying that all diseases come from our emotions. But I could hardly even imagine how true it was. One of my good friends developed cancer after a strong emotional conflict at work. Thank God, everything worked out at the end. We really need to remember what devastating consequences happen from emotional storms and take better care of the people around us.

Be kind, be all sympathy,
For each and every human being
Is forced to fight against himself.

Sri Chinmoy[5]

Fulness of Life

The fulness of life
Lies in dreaming and manifesting
The impossible dreams.

Impossibility always bows
To humanity's patience-mountain.

Sri Chinmoy[6]

In the last two 3100-Mile Races, I was in a very good state by the end: On the one hand, I felt a great inner peace, as if I were at the bottom of the ocean or deep, deep in my heart. On the other hand, I experienced a very powerful energy flowing through my body, often causing goose bumps on my skin. Kausal has described this state as a super receptivity to everything coming from Above and super efficiency on the physical plane. He added that this energy is also healing, and if I could maintain it in everyday life, all my physical weakness would be cured. I asked him how I could keep it? He smiled and said that I should be happy that it happens to me during the Race.

Once when I was running with Galya, we discussed the same question: how to keep this super state at the end of the race in the daily life? And then he said: "It seems that we must continue to live at our maximum capacity." Wow!

Life still conceals many mysteries for us. It is encouraging that we have the power to unveil them with our aspiration. I remember when Virendra set a record of 5:09:30 for the 47-mile race, which lasted for 34 years, Sri Chinmoy told him that if he could maintain the same aspiration and determination as during the race, he would be able to realize God.

If not for my participation in the 3100-Mile Race, I would have not been able to touch this particular state - on the one hand supernatural, on the other hand completely normal. Perhaps most of all, I remember the indomitable inner peace and a kind of special lightness and transparency in my head. As if I had come out from the pressure and influence of all mundane and earthly affairs. And of course, a huge determination to move forward. If we could keep this aspiration-fire in everyday life, we would expect miracles every day, indeed. I am very grateful to the 3100-Mile Race, which - in our movement - reveals the secrets of life. I cannot obtain this just by sitting and meditating.

Needless to say, when you live to your fullest capacity, you are happy to the fullest capacity! Long ago I developed the following formula: the fullness of life lies in movement! When we move, it's easier for the forces from Above to adjust our "trajectory." In physics, for instance, it is known that in order to set a body in motion, it is necessary to apply a force greater than that needed to maintain its motion once it is moving. Absolutely true in our lives! So, in addition to the inner practices, let's move and live to our fullest capacity.

I remember one striking case that happened after a trip to Singapore. When I got home, because of jet lag and the long flight, I found myself with virtually no inspiration to do anything. There were several important projects that needed my attention, but each one looked to be in worse shape than the next. On one project, the client customer would not approve my proposals. On another, there were so many problems that progress seemed impossible. And the third seemed to be stuck in limbo. This doesn't happen to me very often, but when it does, it is usually because of low levels of life-energy. When you feel weak, nothing goes well. The way I felt then, even perfect project management techniques would not help. What I needed was to increase my energy and find some inspiration.

I remembered my best solution to this kind of problem:

If you feel bad or if things aren't going well, put everything out of your mind, lace up your running shoes

*and go out running for an hour or an hour and a half.
You'll feel infinitely happier and you'll find the enthusiasm to get going again.*

And that's just what happened! Running through the
snowy woods, I felt a surge of strength. And I remembered an aphorism of Sri Chinmoy's that said that energy
comes from motion. You probably know a similar prov-
erb: "A rolling stone gathers no moss."

When I got home after my run, it turned out that the
client had approved my proposal, one that would give a
strong boost to the project. When I looked at the project
about which I had so many negative feelings, my attitude changed because I learned about solutions of other
companies that had gone through the same difficulties.
Despite having a hard time during startup, they eventually succeeded. After a few phone calls and some newly
signed contracts, things cleared up on my third project.
Once again I was struck by how much inner power can
help clear away obstacles.

If we just follow our human nature, any difficulties
can compel us to withdraw, hide or isolate ourselves.
And that is just the opposite of what is necessary to re-
store our life force. We need to move! Putting on your
running shoes works every time.

It's interesting how our own mind can block our
progress. Ananda-Lahari walked a lot for the second half
of the race. On day 43, Kausal found his "button." He
began to run and by nine in the evening he had cov-

ered 70 miles. He continued to run until the end of the evening. Kausal said that, as usual, the button was in his mind and in fact everything depended on Ananda-Lahari - whether he wanted to run or not.

When you run on the 3100-Mile Race loop and you are in the "flow" - you are literally in heaven on earth! It was so much written about and so much promised. And where is it? In the middle of an unattractive area in New York – an out-of-the-way neighbourhood. Outwardly, this is no paradise. But inwardly - it is unbelievably beautiful. Therefore many of those who participate in the race feel a strong pull to do it again. Despite the fact that it's extremely hard for the body, despite many other things ... Something tells me that I know how I will spend the next summer.

Searching for the Solutions

Only those who attempt the absurd can achieve the impossible.

Albert Einstein

I believe that every problem has its own solution. If in parallel with the inner cry, mantras, prayers and other spiritual practices, we can help our body to cope with the developing problem, we dramatically increase our speed. The 3100-Mile Race quite often places an unusual task before you that requires extraordinary solutions. Nothing that you knew before seems to help you solve it. I like this experience a lot - especially in retrospect, when I am writing about it – when a solution has been found and the difficult time has passed!

In fact, all my searches during the Race have one aim: to continue to move during 50 days with maximum speed, in various inner states, under all weather conditions.

Kausal taught me a few important things. First, it is necessary to have a diagnosis of your problem. You have to know where you stand. When I hear: "You have to try these pills for the liver; they are super!" Or: "Try this drug; athletes on the US national team take them every day." You have to know whether it is necessary for you. Does the solution match your diagnosis, your problem, your weakness? Often we are the target for a professional marketing, a sales pitch, although there might be absolutely no benefit for our health.

Second - the selection of a remedy must be made according to you as an individual. One demonstration of this happened to me during my second 3100-Mile Race back in 2005. I already knew that I would need an iron supplement. Using a kinesiological test, Pradhan picked up a specific additive for me. When I bought the vitamin before the start, this particular brand was not available.

I bought another brand of the supplement, thinking, "Oh well, all iron is the same." On the third day I was not able to run because of weakness in the legs. Pradhan tested me, and it turned out that this particular iron supplement was blocking me! Since that time, I realized that everyone needs an individual approach. Some things on a base level, I can choose myself. The whole point is whether a particular product or supplement is making you stronger. And of course in critical circumstances, even a fraction of a percent increase or decrease in your strength is crucial.

Anti-heat pill

During 3100-Mile Races I face the challenge of running in extreme weather: hot and humid. High humidity makes physical activity particularly difficult. The fact is that the body tries to reduce the temperature during exercise by sweating. But the higher the humidity, the harder it to "evaporate" the body heat. There comes a time when, due to the high humidity, the cooling system of the body simply breaks down: we cannot maintain a comfortable body temperature and begin to overheat.

My experience tells me that you can take a number of measures, which I call "anti-heat pill," in order to maintain the body's performance in hot and humid weather. This does not make the running easier; it's still extremely difficult to run when the temperature is 36C and the humidity is 90%. But to extend the running and avoid heatstroke is possible.

First, common sense suggests that we protect ourselves from the sun as much as possible and reduce the consumption of energy that our body needs to fight against it. This is not accomplished with just a cap and a t-shirt: we need to choose a material with UV protection. The higher the UV index, the better. Not less than 30. UV material with UV protection can be of different types: just covered with a special chemical composition or with special fibers. Products made with the latter are more expensive, but more durable. In any case, eventually the ability to withstand ultraviolet rays reduces over time, and you need to buy new clothes. Earlier, I wrote about the solution in the form of Solumbra costumes. They perfectly solve the problem of protecting the body from UV rays, and also they have great ventilation and breathability.

Finding relief from the extreme heat in a tub of ice water.
3100-Mile Race in 2006.

In the last few years I also wear the Better Than Naked series of t-shirts by North Face. Very thin, lightweight and breathable. And with UV protection.

It helps to apply sunscreen, also with UV protection of not less than 30, on exposed skin - face, neck, hands and feet. Sunglasses with the same UV protection, and not just plastic lenses, are also very helpful.

Now, about nutrition and supplements: In general, the nutrition strategy in the heat is to minimise foods that require strong digestion, such as proteins. Strong digestion means an excess of acidity in the body. Salads, fruit and vegetables on those days will be a good help. I also wrote about coconut oil, MCT, which is perceived as carbohydrate by the body and remarkably assimilated, supplying the body with fuel, as a real fat. In the long races, such as the 3100-Mile, with a clearly expressed aerobic regimen, the main fuel is fat.

With drinks, the situation is more interesting. Just to drink plenty of water, as it turns out, does not solve the problem. The problem is that this water needs to be assimilated and delivered to the cells of the body. Coconut water does not solve the problem either. Although if you get pure raw coconut water, without preservatives, additives and impurities, it may help.

There are two solutions in my arsenal: Microhydrin (aka Mega Hydrate) and ionized water.

The first additive allows to transport the water into the cells themselves, but is also a powerful antioxidant. The inventor was Patrick Flanagan, who researched various places on earth where life expectancy rose past 100 years. Despite the difference in culture and food, there was one anomaly that united these centenarians: water with a special feature - a high electrical potential. The story of Flanagan's invention is quite an interesting - well worth reading about. To make the story short: Flanagan decided to recreate this living water at home.

Thus Mega Hydrate was born, which allows water to be absorbed and effectively nourish the cells of our body. Otherwise, water can just accumulate in the stomach and not actually reach the cells.

Ionized water also possesses such properties - and more. I will dedicate next chapter to it.

It is also known that in hot weather the body needs an extra supply of potassium and sodium. During the Race, we usually use HeatGuard salt tablets with these micronutrients, which we take every 2-3 hours in hot weather. A Japanese salt called Regidron also works remarkably well. Electrolyte Hydrator Natural Blend by Vega Sport works well, too.

This, briefly, is how I cope with the heat and humidity. Again, extreme conditions do not become comfortable. But you can continue to run without severe side effects in the form of fainting, dehydration and overheating.

Discoveries in Nutrition

Do not be afraid to make mistakes, providing you do not make the same one twice.

Theodore Roosevelt

After having finished nine races, I can assure you that proper diet is able to support, to unfold 100% of your potential given by Mother Nature, while the wrong diet can block your power and condemn you to unnecessary suffering and pain. Thus, it's quite important for the diet to be correct.

Modern medicine has yet to explore and unscramble this field of endurance. However, through my own experience, I can tell you which food products, supplements and vitamins work, and which don't. When I tried to find appropriate experts for my multi-day race preparation back in 2004, I turned to consulting physicians, team doctors and various multi-level representatives. However, the best they could offer was how to keep my peak performance for a 5-day period. The thing is, I needed to keep going for 50 days!

Thus, we have what we have - is a group of people - about 38 runners who have been attempting and finishing the annual Sri Chinmoy Self-Transcendence 3100-Mile Race in New York City for 19 years now - who know better than anyone else what their bodies and spirits need to endure such exertions.

Granted, during the race we are assisted by doctors who can find the 'bug' and suggest how to solve it. Chiropractors help me a lot, too. Strictly speaking, my approach to nutrition and other aspects of fitness was formed slowly from my racing experience and doctors' tips and hints.

Despite the fact that the selection of food, vitamins and supplements is strictly individual, I will try to outline the strategic direction of sports nutrition in the 3100-Mile Race and also to share some of my findings, which can be useful to others.

To start with, I have been a vegetarian for more then 24 years and a follower of the holistic approach in life.

The main idea of holistic nutrition is to preserve the natural integrity of food components, and to avoid products that are not created by nature alone because such products may unbalance our system. And they do! During multi-day races, under great exertion, we reap what we have sown by our lifestyle, when our body fails to perform normally. As you can see, our diet is just the tip of the iceberg. Granted, following a special diet right before and during the race is important, but what really matters is our everyday life and nutrition.

After my early races, I completely refused sugar, all foods containing white flour, and packed juices (with preservatives and artificial additives). They greatly unbalance my system. Imperfect health is too high a price for such food. Sudden weakness, the ebb and flow of energy, heaviness in the stomach, redness on my feet … Both during a race and in my everyday diet, I prefer wholegrain cereals, such as unpolished rice, barley, oat, and my favorite - buckwheat.

During super-long runs, for the first time I heard about the need to support an alkaline state in the body as a guarantee of its long-term performance. Our fatigue indicates that the organism has "soured" and needs time to recover on its own or help to expedite the recovery process. Instead, a special diet that helps to maintain an optimal acid-alkaline balance in the body for a long time is needed.

You are free to explore what products contribute to acidification of the body and what products increase its alkalinity. Here, from a purely practical point of view, vegetarian and vegan diets, in particular, have a great advantage.

As a fundamental and strategic solution of acid-alkaline balance I use ionized water. A special unit produces water with the help of mild electrolysis. Ionized water with its low molecular weight and high reduction potential is an excellent agent for active oxygen absorption. Electrolysis inside the unit not only charges the water with electrons, but also reduces the size of clusters of molecules in the water. Therefore, ionized water penetrates the body cells extremely efficiently.

In practice this means that not only does this super water maintain the water balance in the body, but all the supplements, vitamins and mixtures that you ingest with ionized water work many times more effectively. In particular, as a part of my recovery program, each night, I take a natural vegetarian recovery blend by Vega Sport before going to sleep. Most of the time, I have "new" legs the next morning - after only 4.5 hours of sleep and perhaps a total distance of 100 km the previous day!

As in other cases, here also knowledgeable professional advice is essential to determine the optimum level of alkaline ionized water, which I then select at the ionizer. The thing is that a strong alkaline environment, despite how much it may seem favorable for a tired body, counteracts the acidic environment necessary for effective digestion and functioning of the intestinal tract. Proper digestion is a guarantee of continuous energy supply to the body. You need a golden balance!

My next practical discovery appeared when I had a serious crisis in the middle of the 2015 Race and could only walk most of that day. Kausal suggested a mineral supplement (CellFood) that supplies the muscle cells with oxygen. According to the research, the long-term endurance of the muscles, which means the effective flow of the perform-recover cycle, can be facilitated by oxygen. I suspect this supplement was used to increase stamina in the ultra marathons before! But, as always, he was right. A few days later, my running significantly evened, and the second half of the race was just excellent. I had no recession and no walking-only days in the last 18 days prior to finish. Of course, there were many reasons for that. But we must always focus on what makes us stronger, even in a small measure. The water in the ocean is made out of billions of drops ...

My discoveries in sport nutrition could fill an entire book ... and it did in 2010, when I wrote:

Eat to Run.

Holistic nutrition for the ultra-marathon runner.

Humour Is the Spice of Life

The reasonable man adapts himself to the world: the unreasonable one persists in trying to adapt the world to himself. Therefore all progress depends on the unreasonable man.

George Bernard Shaw

One day, answering the question from the legendary 3100-Mile female runner Suprabha Beckjord, Sri Chinmoy advised her to feel like a little child in order to find new energy to move forward. Indeed, kids do not walk - they constantly run, jump and fidget. And it all happens with laughter, squeals and smiles. When they are not sleeping, children embody a whirlwind of energy and fun! Well, we adults need to approach this tsunami of energy from the other side: to try to create a good mood, smile and ... try to become a child. That's when our energy comes spontaneously. All my good days with best miles were distinguished by a higher contents of humour in my blood and the amazing combination of inner peace and outer fun.

We have a favorite musical group at the Race - Enthusiasm Awakeners. A group of girls comes to the track for half an hour every morning in all weather to inspire us by singing Sri Chinmoy's songs, many of which he wrote for them specifically for the 3100-Mile Race. We also have a tradition that Grahak began in 2007: We perform short funny sketches for them. Performing them makes us laugh, and sometimes the girls laugh too. This year we put on a few scenes with Galya. Here is one:

- Hi, Galya.

- Hi, Stutisheel.

- You know that Japanese do not eat fat food and live longer than Canadians and Americans?

- I also know that the French are fond of fatty foods and still live longer than Americans and Canadians.

- So what's the conclusion?

- It seems that you can eat anything you want. What kills is the English language.

Before we performed, I had been working for a few days with pain in one of my joints. Despite the ointments, supplements and treatments, it would not go away. But as soon as we performed the scene, and everyone laughed - wham! A shiver passed through my body, and the joint stopped hurting. This pain never returned.

What kills is the English language - sketch with Galya.

I already wrote that bright, positive emotions produce a strong alkaline reaction in the body, which is far superior to the effect of all known antioxidants. So, even on the physical plane, humour alleviates our problems.

Often in the morning, when we had to find new strength to finally wake up and run forward, many of us would read the summary of new jokes and funny stories that we got from our friends. After half an hour of laughing on the go, everything settled into place.

Below are my favourites jokes – and also real funny stories from the Race during previous years:

Some atheists come to God. An Angel says: "My Lord, two atheists have come to see you". God thinks for a while and says: "Tell them that I am absent."

❦

A blind man with his seeing-eye dog goes into a store. Suddenly he takes the dog by its tail and swings it around above his head. A scared shopkeeper asks: "May I help you?" The man answers: "No, thanks. I am just looking around."

- I suppose sometimes you think that I am a perfect idiot!

- Oh, no, no. Nobody is perfect.

Pranjal somehow got a red stain on the back of his T-shirt. Many people wondered about it because it looked like a bullet wound. When I finally asked him about it, he answered, "I guess I'd better change my shirt because even a policeman asked me: "Are you okay, sir? I can see that you are wounded"

We were running with Igor and I was saying that almost a week of life in our great Race was over. We have seen all the nuances, I said. The only thing which we have not seen yet are massive fire engines with flashing lights, loud sirens and a huge American flag behind. I was telling him that firemen are heroes in the United States. And Igor says: Yes, probably you have to be a very rich guy to buy a fire engine.

Every morning Rupantar picks up Ashprihanal from his house first. One day when a sleepy Ashprihanal came out the house, Rupantar asked: Hi! How are you? Ashprihanal got into the car and in only 10 seconds answered: I am okay. You see? 10 seconds! Good reaction. The funniest thing in this story is that when Rupantar told him about it later, Ashprihanal said he didn't remember anything.

Ashprihanal confessed that he has a psychological issue, which he calls a "speech defect." Over the thirteen years that he has been in the 3100-Mile Race, running for one and a half months every year, he developed the habit of talking while moving. When he is in Helsinki, he often catches himself asking his friend to have a cup of coffee together passing by him. Only afterwards he realizes that he didn't get an answer.

It's all about Galya. … This night he was determined to sleep in his bed and not on a chair or in the bathroom as he often does. So, after taking the shower he finally made it to his bed… only to find himself sitting on the bed at 4:40 the next morning!

Surasa is running with a cabbage wrap around her

ankle to cure her shin splints. She stops at a fence to do some stretching. Ashprihanal runs by and comments:

– I wouldn't advise you to do so much stretching.

– ??

– The cabbage might attract rabbits, and that would make it worse!

Just before the race started, Rupantar said that our bathrooms would have locks on. Because the race happens to be in a public place, there are many people around, especially on weekends, who come to play soccer, etc. Rupantar told each runner the combination – "777 – very easy. You just have to turn to one digit." I said, "Okay, if there are any problems, we'll let you know." Right after that Asprihanal said, "It just feels like we have something very precious in those bathrooms! That's why the locks are on."

An Effective Relaxation

At times,
Relaxation plays the role
Of our true saviour.

Sri Chinmoy[7]

What I write is primarily connected to the multi-day endurance running. Clearly, during 2-mile races, 5Ks, half marathons, and even marathons, one strives to maintain maximum speed, making the whole race experience very intense. But the longer the race, the more important the spontaneous and endless flow of energy that moves one forward becomes. I noticed some interesting conditions that help "catch" that flow.

Ashprihanal Aalto, who is the world record holder for the 3100-Mile Race, is often asked about the secret to his extraordinary performance. His response depends on his mood. This year, he repeatedly emphasised the ability to relax. He has a very interesting style to prove how important this is: he manages to run pretty fast, despite using his arms separately from the rest of the body. He moves them with no relevance to his steps ... But the fact is: when things are going well, he runs very lightly and naturally, with the inimitable waving arms. The more his arms move randomly, the better mood he has and the better performance. And vice versa. When he had some very difficult days before yet another finish in 2013, he walked with his hands in the pockets of his running shorts.

Following Ashprihanal, I can confirm that it is possible to make a maximum of miles, when you are able to relax the body. To remove all blocks, you can say. And then the energy flows with no obstacles.

It's a paradox, isn't it? To run the most, one must relax the most. That, by the way, fits perfectly the picture of my state at maximum efficiency: inner calmness, complete peace, plus outer intensity, which manifests itself without tension, naturally.

I saw different approaches to covering the distance of 3100 miles. Due to the cultural peculiarities of countries such as Germany or Austria, the runners showed great discipline and performed the schedule almost in seconds. And when it was necessary to meet a certain number of laps at a milestone, you could see their tension and their policy of "paying any price to achieve the goal." I admired their iron will and also tried this approach. But in the end, I adopted Ashprihanal's method: Although I have milestones, I try not to "over-push" myself and run with as much relaxation as possible. I know that eventually I will do so more miles. And when I over-push myself, especially in the evening in order to make a certain number of laps, it seems that I am burning some special reserve in the muscles. Then my legs ache at night, and I have a bad sleep. I do not recover completely even by the next morning. It might even provoke a walking day.

Ashprihanal and his arms.

The ability to effectively relax is important not only in endurance running but in daily life, as well. During the more than 30 years of my running career, I "outlasted" many friends and training associates, who in time, for various reasons, quit running and sports altogether. This was, above all, due to overtraining and an inability to relax and recover. For an athlete, the most effective relaxation means the most effective recovery (and assimilation of the previous load). Here, meditation plays a great role for me. I had some very good experiences, when all the muscle soreness was taken away after deep meditation! I believe this practice contributes a lot to my "new" legs every morning at the 3100-Mile Race.

Also, an important role in the forming of my approach was played by my father Dmytro Lebediev. He is the two-times European champion in marathon distance in the age group 70-74 (EVACS 2012, EVACS 2014) and bronze medalist of the World Championship WMA 2015 (marathon time - 3:25:39). He usually chooses one major marathon per year and never chases after the number of marathons. He prepares intensively and performs perfectly. The rest of the year he trains and competes in shorter distances "just for pleasure."

*Dmytro Lebediev crossing the marathon finish line
at the World Master Athletic Championship - 3:25:39.
France, 2015.*

The Best Personal Example

Because your own strength is unequal to the task, do not assume that it is beyond the powers of man; but if anything is within the powers and province of man, believe that it is within your own compass also.

Marcus Aurelius

One of the most significant achievements in my life due to the 3100-Mile Race probably was that in the winter of 2015 my daughter Alakakananda suddenly expressed the wish to run a marathon, 26.2 miles, by the end of that year. She requested me to train her and monitor the progress. What a surprise that was! I remember all the times I tried motivating her to run when she was a child, and when she got a little older, she started to protest, saying, dad, do not push me. Eventually I let her go her own way. She practiced yoga from time to time, swam, but there was no constant presence of sport in her life. And then – a lighting out of the blue! It is difficult to find a better motivator, perhaps, then a personal example. Just 10 starts in 3100-Mile Race were necessary…

However, I immediately felt that this was not solely the result of my example. As usual, Sri Chinmoy was waiting for the right moment to sow the seed. And now it began to sprout. I clearly saw his look and heard his words: "And now you train her well".

Alakananda registered for a marathon in Honolulu, Hawaii, in December of that year. The first scheduled workout was started in April. I had to make her a marathoner "from scratch". Before that, she could barely run two miles without being out of breath… I outlined a strategic plan for her launch into the orbit and began to prepare a detailed training schedule every month.

My second shock was how dutifully she followed the training plan. Knowing that discipline is not her forte, I was truly amazed when she tried not to miss a single workout and perform all the scheduled tasks.

Some of my very familiar hobbies and topics emerged in her life as well: a Garmin watch, good running shoes, running outfits, nice sunglasses, and sports nutrition.

During the last month before the start she trained six times a week, running a hundred kilometers per week. The first milestone half marathon she ran in 2:18, second – in 2:11. But the main thing was that she fell in love with running! She became more active, and discovered a big positive drive. I've heard her say things like, "dad, what was I doing before this?". For me, it is obvious that such transformation is impossible without a touch from Above...

Upon learning about Alakananda's progress, one of the 3100-Mile Runners wrote me a nice letter saying that she already became a winner, even before the start.

Honolulu marathon itself, although colorful, turned out to be quite difficult. High humidity right at the start, even as early as 5 am, and the temperature steadily increasing up to 30C, especially after the sunrise. And the most difficult part ... 35 000 runners!

In such extreme conditions Alakananda predictably could not reach the scheduled pace, and, around

Walking with daughter during her tough marathon part. Hawaii, 2015.

the 30K mark, she hit the wall... The following 7K she walked, and only at the end she found strength to run to the finish line. Her estimated (and trained for) finish time was 4:30. Actual - 5:46. Let me tell you, the experience is not for the weak! However, after the recovery period, I noticed a familiar spirit: although she didn't say it outwardly, we understood each other perfectly. One day she will come back and perform in this marathon as expected!

Going Beyond Limits

The only way of discovering the limits of the possible
is to venture a little way past them into the
impossible.

Arthur C. Clarke

f a classical medicine doctor, an urologist for example, saw me in the down days, he would prescribe bed rest, monitoring, medications, and much more. But usually, it takes a day or two for the crisis to pass, and I already run with a speed above average. Is it not a miracle? It is a working of Grace from Above. During the Race, everything works out in an interesting way. Very often you catch yourself thinking that classical medicine would be just "resting." In fact, sometimes our track doctors were surprised at our conditions and performances as well. Even if the case is complicated and appears to be difficult to solve, the next day everything is miraculously resolved without any visible outer assistance.

After my severe crisis when I picked my speed back

up to "flying", Ashprihanal noticed that in the Race I only have two states: "on" and "off". And if it is "off", it is a really major breakdown and I can look just scary.

On the day 31 of the Race, I was having the weakest day this year, and Utpal interviewed me. This coincided with some roadworks on our route: huge machines, a lot of workers, the smell of asphalt and tar ...

"It is still shocking, no matter how many times you've done the Race before. Of course you can say it extends your limits of everything. Of accepting, of transcending, of patience, of everything.

From the outer point of view it is what it is. I feel though that we (the runners) have enough power to dive deep within, and to not be distracted so much. This is the case when you live in the heart. When you are in your own inner world. Than it is not a distraction.

I love to say, the divine and the earthly always go hand in hand. You cannot escape anything. I believe we have enough inner power, enough inner strength to come victorious out of all our difficulties.

There is no usual 3100-Mile Race. Every Race is unique. Maybe your previous experiences can help you a little bit to avoid some major mistakes. Otherwise, you cannot predict what will happen. You just need to be receptive and never give up. All the usual things that can save your life."

During the years of participation in the 3100-Mile Race, the most special moments took place while going beyond the limits of your capabilities and past achievements. The first 70 mile day, the first day with only one break (there was a huge burst of energy that I felt), the first result with the finish time of faster than 51 days, a personal best of 48 days ...

Every time I surpassed inclement weather or heat and transcended the limits of my human nature, some special subtle energy flowed, causing tingling in my skin. It was always accompanied by a feeling of flight and freedom. It is amazing how this could take place during one of the most extreme races in the whole world!

I want to especially highlight two runners, who also happen to be my good friends (they also held the finish line tape at my finish in 2015) - Ashprihanal Aalto and Galya Balatskyy.

Ashprihanal and I met at my first 3100-Mile Race in 2004. Ever since, we are always very happy to see each other in the summer, "same place, same time"

At this year's start we all had a special feeling towards Ashprihanal: later it formulated in a phrase: "he is chosen". We were all in "shock" from his miles at the beginning of the race. It seemed that even he himself was a little surprised. But gradually his 140 or more laps a day (123 km) became a commonplace ... I must say, the mind quickly gets used to everything. However, inwardly, we had a special feeling towards this unique and humble postman from Helsinki for the duration of the entire race. Being a leader in the race, and even more so being focused on the world record meant that one is always under the watchful eyes of both divine and undivine forces alike. And of course, it is always a big pressure. Therefore, inwardly we tried supporting him in his coping with the task by sending our good will and prayers. As well as by outer support, like cheers, humor, and jokes. Often his responses were lightning-fast, due to his sharp tongue. He said that in the past, the start was usually very good, but at the end, something always went wrong. This time, it turned out that he is able to run practically with maximum speed almost the entire Race. Special blessings from Above! And he more then deserved it, for his 13 starts in the 3100-Mile Race.

As he passed milestone after milestone with new achievements, it became clear that a new record was imminent. It felt like a sense of fatality, in a good way.

On the day of his record finish on the forty-first day, I was thinking how would I be able to capture his state in a short interview. But everything turned out perfectly by itself. He caught up with me on his pre last lap, and I just needed to grab my iPhone, turn on the camera and record the conversation on his very last lap before the finish - awesome! Maybe it will become a historical interview with time... We realized that him and I participated in nine Races. Ashprihanal also said that he witnessed how Alakananda grew up, every year. When she first appeared at the Race in 2005 as my helper, she was 13 years old. In the middle of the last lap a police car with flashing lights appeared out of the blue and accompanied Ashprihanal moving along the carriageway up to the finish line. Before the last turn I felt particularly intense joy, a familiar energy, as if in the presence of Sri Chinmoy. I felt how much he is proud of Ashprihanal's achievement. I told Ashprihanal - he nodded. And then I let him run with the Race flag to the finish line - to meet fans and many photographers.

Ashprihanal finished the 3100-Mile Race this year in 40 days 9 hours 6 minutes and 21 seconds. He set a new world record, surpassing the 9-year-old Madupran's achievement by more than a day.

I was very lucky to be with Ashprihanal during his last lap - for a few days after that, I was under impression and on the rise from intense joy I felt. It turns out that finishes of the other runners you often experience more intense than even your own.

Ashprihanal's finish with the new 3100-Mile Race world record - 40 days + 9:06:21.

By the way, Madhupran sent a very touching congratulatory message to Ashprihanal. Here are some excerpts:

I am tremendously happy for you - you deserve the world record! Your constancy and focus is spectacular. I have always admired you for your ease. You run like a feather. This is self-transcendence par excellence. You are the greatest! I am happy for you with all my heart.
Madhupran Wolfgang Schwerk

Enjoying the ride around the Race course after setting the world record.

During the race, we ran with Galya, if not a thousand miles, then maybe a little less than that. He is truly a runner from God. A part of his training for 3100-Miles was participation in several 24 hour races, including the world championship in Italy, where many took his autographs, for he is famous in elite sport circles for his extraordinary achievements. In the 2015 Race, he set a new Ukrainian record, a new record for the former Soviet countries - I think you can easily expand the countries geography, because he achieved absolute third place in the 3100-Mile ranking. By his result of 43 days + 17:39:59, he surpassed all previous results of Ashprihanal to date. Moreover, he holds a unique record of completing ALL 43 days with 70 or more miles per day (and even the very last one!). This would be very difficult to plan, and even more difficult to beat! Neither Ashprihanal nor Madhupran could achieve this - no one else in the world.

Among his special achievements this year was a very strong result for the split of 1300 miles - 17 days +15:36:22. In the entire ultra-marathon history, including a dedicated race for 1300 miles, only 10 runners in the world were able to meet the 18 day deadline. And Galya's result is the seventh fastest - in the split!

I would like to lift the veil a little, because only few people realized what risks Galya faced at the start of 3100-Miles in 2015.

His main problem was a knee injury, that he developed a year ago. He ran (and won) 24H races with some pain, but when he did the MRI, it turned out that he had a tear of the meniscus and the Baker's cyst. Classical medicine recommendation was to proceed with the operation. Generally, athletes with such a diagnosis are not allowed to run not only 3100-Miles, but to compete in any race whatsoever. But Galya had a plan: if something were to happen to his knee, he would get on a plane and fly to Minneapolis to a doctor who is able to insert the meniscus in a non surgical way. Then Dr. Kumar told him to wear two knee pads, since the knees are the paired organs, and buy pain killers just in case. Overall, he felt a lot of tension before the start. Thank God, that risk was not triggered.

When it comes to world-class achievements, as it was in his case, the border between fanaticism and faith is very thin. If you use common sense, then you might as well forget about the 3100! But he felt the same way I did - that it is necessary to follow your heart, and that there were certain assurances from Above. A very fine line ... But we also must pay tribute to Dr. Kausal, who is well-knowledgable in traditional medicine, and, at the same time, he is a super Ayurvedic doctor and a specialist in subtle energies. Upon his arrival at the track around day 40 of the Race, he said that the long monotonous jogging only strengthens the knee. If he only said that to Galya a little earlier!

Also Galya had a problem with his teeth. A day before the start he had bad toothache and also the seal came out. He managed to visit the doctor and seal was reinstalled. After yet another seal came out, which could not be fixed before the start ... He also had a couple of inflamed teeth, which caused problems. For this case there was a plan also: within ten minutes of the Race course there is a private dental clinic. He thought he would run extra miles at the beginning, and then drive to a doctor. But this problem never developed either. Only for the first two weeks he was a little nervous, as was everyone else. Because of the teeth problems Galya's breakfast consisted of baby food, which he was not very fond of.

Despite all this, the finish happened. Joyful and unforgettable. With a super time, too! According to him, "it was impossible to do more, but less - I could not."

Cake for the champion at Galya's finish.

When you run with such amazing people here at the Race, it is not life, but a paradise. I was very lucky to see the willpower of both Ashprihanal and Galya; and learn from them. Life is beautiful!

Gratitude

Gratitude has to be
A universal currency

Sri Chinmoy[8]

By the end of the Race you are filled with gratitude, especially to the Creator, the Supreme, because you realize and feel that He cares for you so much. You realize that you run and move forward only because you have been given the power from Above. The 3100-Mile Race is too long and unpredictable to finish it on our own, very limited, human strength.

Also, you experience a special feeling of gratitude for all who care about you, watch the progress of the Race, send words of support. It is exceptionally nice to feel that you have a big family all over of the globe. It is a nectar to the heart as well as to the body.

Only One Power

*The difficult is that which can be done immediately,
the impossible that which takes a little longer.*

George Santayana

Below I would like to quote my words after my finish
of the 3100-Mile Race on August 3rd, 2015.

"I would like to thank the race directors. The
undying enthusiasm from morning till evening, for so
many days, unbelievable! The cooks, unimaginable!
Better and better from year to year. I don't know how
they do better, but they do better every year. I wish to
thank the Enthusiasm Awakeners singing group, and
specially their performance on 4th of July. I would like
to thank my family, Alakananda and Atandra. My fellow
runners - they are the best people in the world! And of
course my deepest gratitude goes to my Guru, Sri Chinmoy.

It was not easy, especially during the first half. I
believe there were many factors. I faced a few crises. In

those days, it seemed as though I was running a different race in a different place...

The second half of the race was pretty even, pretty stable, and pretty joyful. So this is a very good conclusion to my 11th start and 9th finish.

I remember one day when Ashprihanal finished. I shared his last lap with him. For me, it was an unforgettable experience. I was inundated with happiness, power, peace, and everything. Ashprihanal finished on a Friday and the next day was the weekend with a handball tournament. Saturday and Sunday were inundated with so many people and so much activity. Despite all that, it was one of the most blissful weekends for me. It happened because of this inner power that came to me because of the finish of my good friend.

Last lap before Ashprihanal's finish.

The answer is in inner poise and inner power. We just have to cry for it and to be receptive to it.

If you look at pictures of all the finishers - they are so happy, unimaginably happy. It is not earthly happiness. It is something heavenly, deep, and intense, and, at the same time, sublime. It is so powerful and divine. I believe happiness spreads from here over the inner channels. The message spreads out of happiness, peace, and transcendence.

I was impressed by one Sri Chinmoy's sayings that I received in a support letter:

There is only one power, one divine power. There is one power that works inside the whole universe, not two powers.[9]

Only one power that is behind everything and everybody. Sometimes I could see the play of this power in people and behind events. It is always present."

Secrets Revealed

That which does not kill us, makes us stronger.

Friedrich Nietzsche

The 3100-Mile Race code is cracked – the secret is revealed! The secret, as always, is very simple. It lies in the number of 5649. This is the number of laps needed to complete the 3100-Mile Race. And as it turned out, everyone who does so many laps experiences incredible happiness that is not attainable in ordinary life. I think this is the biggest secret of the 3100-Mile Race. Although we say that experiences are like diamonds scattered along the way, in reality, when I recall my finishes and finishes of other runners, when you approach this number of 5649 laps, something incredible happens. Such intense joy and fulfillment come to the fore. Awesome! I was very fortunate to experience this state nine times in my life - on my nine finishes in 3100-Mile Race.

I try to remember my previous attempts at breaking

the 5649 code.

My first Race happened in **2004**. It was a bright finish at 10am on day 54. The entire run was definitely a shock to the body: constant back pain, pain in the feet, a lot of other things. A memorable Race, for sure. But, nevertheless, 5649 laps I completed, and even at the finish line I already knew that I would be back to run many, many more times. I said it out loud, and many of those who were present at my finish were shocked. How is it possible?

The result of my first 3100-Mile Race - 53 days + 3:57:38. 34 years old.

My first finish in 3100-Miles - 2004.

The weather during my second race in **2005** was very hot. I barely survived to the last days. Applying great efforts, I was able to run a little bit and finish on 55th day by running and not walking. A few days after my finish, on her birthday, my daughter received a spiritual name from Sri Chinmoy - Alakananda. The most beloved heart-river of Mother India ...

The result - 54 days + 6:41:55.

Finish with daughter - 2005.

2006. This was the first year when my wife and daughter both helped me at the Race. Directly on the track during the Race Sri Chinmoy gave the spiritual name to my wife - Atandra. God-seeker and God-lover...

The result - 54 days + 4:24:41

2007 - the last Race which Sri Chinmoy visited ... And this was the first year when I met the initial deadline of 51 days. I remember how fast I was running on the last day – I felt incredible happiness and flight. An ocean of energy! The code has been successfully broken. And then on my finish, Sri Chinmoy wrote our name-song - Stutisheel, Alakananda, Atandra. Now it is sung every time I finish. It was a very bright, memorable Race. It is clear that when you get such rich experiences, you want to come back next year to reap the harvest again.

The result - 50 days + 12:21:25

Sri Chinmoy's visit to my finish - 2007.

The year 2008. I improved my time by about an hour. As a result of this run, I wrote a book "Where dreams come true".

The result - 50 days + 11:19:46

2009 clearly imprinted in my memory. The first time I performed on a decent level – my finish time was 48 days. Almost the entire Race I had a super positive drive, and for the first time I reached 70 miles per day. I remember at the finish I asked Alakananda: "And that's it?" Race went by very quickly. And, of course, I was very happy.

The result - 48 days + 12:42:46

2010 - The tragic year for me. I got an injury. A torn ligament in the knee. I stopped on day 24 after covering 1386 miles because of my incapacity to even walk... Atandra, seeing my condition, got a shock of her life and disappeared from 3100-Mile Race for 5 years. This was the first time on the 3100-Mile track when I was on crutches, and as a spectator... However, I had no doubt that I will start next year. My joint successfully healed

and became even stronger. I tested it in the 6 day race in the spring of the next year.

The very last lap before stop in 3100-Mile Race due to the torn ligament. 2010

2011 was a difficult race. I would even call it my hardest finish in 3100. For the last three weeks I had an inflamed sciatic nerve, and a very tricky shin splint on the side of my leg. Ashprihanal was able to determine that this was the shin splint only by the end of the Race, because he had that once, too. These two injuries did not really evolve, but did not go away either - they were on duty one after the other, without any break in between. I remember when I woke up in the morning on the day of my finish and realized that the next day I would not manage to the starting line... It was a difficult finish on a late rainy evening on day 53, but, nevertheless, the code has been broken yet again. 5649. The result - 52 days + 16:19:18

Late rainy night finish - 2011.

2012. At the end of the Race I got yet another shin splint and had to walk for the last 5 days. When I recovered and started doing 65 miles per day again, the finish line was looming large ... And then I was switched off by the full moon influence. My hopes to meet the deadline and finish faded away, along with any motivation to move forward... The last days were just terrible...I didn't meet the 52 days deadline, that was once again reestablished by organisers, and finished with 2865 miles.

2013. The last few years prior to this year have been pretty severe, and in 2013 I took a break to better understand and assimilate past experiences. It was the year of my first Ironman. I did a lot of speed training. When I started in 3100-Mile Race next year, I set a personal best.

First Ironman finish.

Year 2014. A new personal best! I improved my previous achievement from 5 years ago. Many interesting discoveries, and most importantly - I have strengthened the belief in myself that I still can do a lot.

The result - 48 days + 3:57:19, 44 years old.

3100-Mile Race finish in 2014 with new personal best - 48 days + 3:57:19.

2015. 9th finish. The code was broken in 51 days. Once again, a miracle happened and an all pervasive feeling of happiness came. Needless to say that when you are happy, you need nothing else. You do not need the advice or even an opinion from others - whether you do right thing or not. When you are happy, you become self-sufficient. No, rather, God-sufficient.

The result - 50 days + 12:52:49

2015 finish. Finish tape is hold by my 3100 friends -
Galya and Ashprihanal.

Everyone experiences 3100-Miles in his/her own way, but to get access to the happiness we need to apply a lot of sincere effort. There is no shortcut out of this circle, and these 5649 laps. Just take everything in until the end. And then everything opens..

The Global Picture of Life

Whether you think you can, or you think you can't -
you're right

Henry Ford

I believe that the seeds that were planted during the Race in the inner world in the hearts of runners, as well as people who watched and sympathized with the Race, will germinate and bear fruits for a long time to come.

After the official end of the 3100-Mile Race I asked Bipin, one of the Race Directors, how this year's event looked from the organizers side. He said that the collective consciousness of the runners was very high. And, perhaps, this helped with two world and four personal records. What a good Race!

Despite the fact that the first half of the race was hard for me, I evened out my running in the second part. Regardless of the result, each finish in 3100-Mile Race is a whole new era, a huge milestone in the life of a runner. And if you look at the intensity and variety of experiences we go through, it can be as valuable as, perhaps, a few lifetimes.

I think the Creator definitely has a "plan" for each runner. And the plan is very good! But it may not always show itself within a small period of time, even the 50 days of the 3100-Mile Race, for instance. At minimum, you need a few years to get the insight of a global picture of life, the progress-plan.

It may seem that for Kaneenika, for example, the Race was filled with difficulties and suffering ... I definitely feel that her brilliant victories are still ahead. From my experience of staring the Race 11 times, I can say that all the runners have had difficult times, cases, sometimes even very difficult years.

Madhupran, for example, tried to set a world record several times. In 2004, his spine nerve got inflamed and absolutely nobody could help him with it. Sri Chinmoy and the best sports doctors and masseurs at our disposal visited the Race track every day. Yet, Madhupran was still not able to run and was compelled to walk. But he did not give up and returned to the track in 2006 and finally set the world record.

For Ashprihanal, the last two years before his triumphant finish were some dramatic races! A few times he received heat strokes and found himself in a critical condition under the dropper. At that time, he was overtaken by two runners just a few days before his finish who pushed him to the third place, and he fell into a deep depression and finished by walking. He walked a few days before the finish, feeling completely down, with his hands in his shorts pockets. But he didn't give up, and came back in 2015 to set a new world record!

First three Races were quite difficult for me also. I reached the "flight" state and the feeling of freedom during the 3100-Mile Race only in 2007. Only at my fourth race I met the original 51 day deadline for the first time.

There is a progress-plan for everybody. The impression I get is that we do not appreciate anything that comes to us easily. We do not impart due importance. I see that through self-transcendence all the difficult experiences we can end up in immense happiness and great progress.

A Mystery of 3100-Miles

Apparently there is nothing that cannot happen today.

Mark Twain

For some reason, the 2015 3100-Mile Race was a completely unpredictable, and I would even say, with some lack of logic and common sense. It blew everybody's mind away completely. I even thought that the more I run 3100-Mile Race, the less I understand what's going on …

Sometimes in the morning I felt hopeless: not enough sleep, weak legs, etc. But by dinner time I was fully functional, and reached 65 miles or more by the end of the day. Sometimes it was also vice versa: a good mood and shape in the morning, but after the first break in the afternoon it was difficult to wake up, I had no tone, and I had to continue with walking…

Although, a few months after the finish I got a better understanding of the reasons for my hard days. In particular, one reason was very poor energy in the apartment where I slept. I spent about 5 hours per night there, but due to the heavily blocked energy, I never recovered as expected. Even when I managed to solve the various problems of the first half of the run, bad energy of my nightly resting place, as a background factor, lowered my overall performance ...

Even more puzzles surfaced about the preparations for the Race. After the finish, I heard interesting details about both Surasa and Ashprihanal. Surasa only trained for 50 minutes per day, and not even every day. And Ashprihanal only ran a marathon distance once, as a preparation for the race. During other days he followed the formula "not to over train before the start." And to work on his speed, all he did was the 2 mile race every Saturday. Nothing special. And in the Race these two both set world records! Then I thought, why should I kill myself with 70K runs and speed workouts at my maximum heart-rate?!

Woman's 3100-Miles world record, performed by Surasa from Austria. 2015

In fact, it seems to me that the race is so unpredictable because we try to understand it with our limited mind and common sense. We were taught at school that one plus one equals two. In life, this is not always the case. And at the 3100-Mile Race - even more so. Here, although important, physical condition does not completely determine the performance outcome.

Once runners had the opportunity to ask Sri Chinmoy a question each, and he wanted to make a book out of his answers.

I asked him then: what actually happens during the 3100-Mile Race?

We never got the answers, and the book never came out …

For me, it is obvious that all of the events that manifest in each of the Races, are rooted deeply into the inner world of causes, often unknown to us. We can have glimpses of them sometimes. For instance, we all felt, right from the first day, that this edition of the Race is going to be very special and that Ashprihanal was on a "special mission." It was clear that he was "chosen".

This is the most unpredictable and mystic thing about the 3100-Mile Race. This is a very inner, spiritual race. It is run by a "Heavenly manager." And it's a great thing! Many times I found myself thinking about how wonderful it is that the human management is not the governance crown. Otherwise we would have a catastrophe after catastrophe …

In my case, I still feel the need for intensive training and good preparation for the Race. It is my homework, and if I did not do it, I would get a bad mark for my performance. But only God knows what will happen during the Race. As I've said, my attitude is to do the maximum I am capable of under any circumstances, and to simply continue to move forward. Even if it's at a snail's pace.

Several times during the Race, I had a vision that there is a huge funnel that is unwound by the 3100-Mile runners. Perhaps this funnel is used by the divine powers to transform the problems of the world ... But what actually happens on the track, God alone knows.

A couple of days around day 20, when I was walking I was re-listening Dan Brown's "The Lost Symbol," in which the author traditionally very skillfully interweaves facts with his artistic speculation about the foundation of the US capital, Washington. Pyramids, secret societies, secret knowledge, the circle of initiates... I was prompted to see the similarity with our race.

Only a few people know that here, in the outwardly unattractive and, I can even say, unfavourable area of New York, lies the sacred golden lap. It may happen that at this lap the level of transformation of human nature and the power to influence the world as a whole can equal or even exceed the similar things of places of worship, churches, monasteries and other sacred places. Few people realize what happens here, what epochal things take place, aimed at establishing peace in the world. Few people realize, even among the participants. In Dan Brown's words, here is the "portal" to another dimension.

Despite the fact that the deep and global plan of the 3100-Mile Race, that was laid by Sri Chinmoy's Vision, is still behind the veil, - with each start, with every Race edition, more and more experience-particles form into a huge mosaic. Outwardly it is definitely the most difficult Race. But inwardly it is very powerful and extremely joyful. It still conceals a lot of mysteries and waits for many more self-giving runners.

Perhaps you?

3100-Mile Race start in 2008 - a rare case when the first lap we ran all together.

3100-Mile Race Ranking (1997-2015)

#	Time: day+h:min:sec	Name, age, country	Average, miles per day	Year
1	40+09:06:21	Ashprihanal Aalto, 44, Finland	76.776	2015
2	41+08:16:29	Madhupran W.Schwerk, 50, Germany	74.983	2006
3	42+17:39:59	Galya Vladimir Balatskyy, 43, Ukraine	72.542	2015
4	43+10:36:39	Grahak Cunningham, 35, Australia	71.363	2012
5	44+06:10:42	Vasu Duzhiy, 49, Russia	70.049	2015
6	44+06:58:10	Sarvagata Ukrainskii, 41, Ukraine	69.996	2014
7	44+13:32:04	Ayojan Stojanovich, 43, Serbia	69.566	2006
8	45+02:30:07	Igor Mudryck, 37, Ukraine	68.733	2011
9	45+03:44:21	Atmavir Petr Spacil, 30, Czech Republic	68.655	2009
10	45+13:49:54	Pranab Vladovich, 32, Slovakia	68.022	2008
11	45+16:45:21	Yuri Trostenyuk, 50, Ukraine	67.840	2015
12	46+17:02:06	Istvan Sipos, 39, Hungary	66.367	1998
13	47+04:10:35	Hans-Jurgen Schlotter, 43, Germany	65.717	2006
14	47+04:19:49	Pranjal Milovnik, 38, Slovakia	65.709	2010
15	47+05:39:58	Edward Kelley, 41, USA	65.628	1998
16	48+03:57:19	Stutisheel Lebedev, 44, Ukraine	64.366	2014
17	48+04:13:54	Smarana Puntigam, 36, Austria	64.351	2007
18	48+04:18:38	Namitabha Arsic, 35, Serbia	64.364	2000
19	48+05:02:44	Kuranga M.Peel, 37, Austria	64.305	2004
20	48+08:22:16	Pushkar C. Mullauer, 40, Switzerland	64.121	2012
21	49+07:52:01	Surasa Mairer, 56, Austria	62.848	2015
22	49+14:25:37	Ananda-Lahari Zuscin, 31, Slovakia	62.502	2006
23	49+14:30:54	Suprabha Beckjord, 42, USA	62.494	1998
24	50+02:44:08	Rimas Jakelaitis, 47, Lithuania	61.862	2002
25	50+03:36:01	Trishul Cherns, 42, Canada	61.815	1999
26	50+03:55:08	Sarah Barnett, 38, Australia	61.802	2014
27	50+11:52:27	Diganta Adhikari Pobitzer, 26, Austria	61.395	2006
28	50+13:48:57	Sopan Tsvetan Tsekov, 25, Bulgaria	61.297	2006
29	50+15:06:04	William Schel, 60, Scotland	61.233	2014
30	51+09:54:59	Nidhruvi Zimmerman, 47, Austria	60.299	2013
31	51+10:04:37	Arpan DeAngelo, 52, USA	60.291	2004
32	51+12:12:13	Nirbhasa Magee, 35, Irland	60.187	2015
33	51+12:30:32	Jayasalini Olga Abramovskikh, 33, Russia	60.173	2014
34	51+13:17:32	Dharbhasana Lynn, New Zealand	60.134	2010
35	53+09:03:25	Pradeep Hoogakker, 33, Netherlands	58.080	2011
36	54+11:34:37	Abichal Watkins, 47, Wales	56.902	2008
37	54+14:26:40	Baladev Pavol Saraz, 33, Slovakia	56.777	2009
38	54+15:39:14	Ratin Boulton, 31, Australia	56.725	2004

Ranking by Number of Finishes

	Men	
1	Ashprihanal Aalto, Finland	13
2	Pranjal Milovnik, Slovakia	10
3	Stutisheel Lebedev, Ukraine	9
4	Atmavir Spacil, Czech Republic	8
5	Smarana Puntigam, Austria	7
6	Namitabha Arsic, Serbia	5
7	Ananda-Lahari Zuscin, Slovakia	5
8	Abichal Watkins, Wales	5
9	Pranab Vladovich, Slovakia	4
10	Madhupran W.Schwerk, Germany	4
11	Sarvagata Ukrainskii, Ukraine	4
12	Grahak Cunningham, Australia	4
13	Diganta Adhikari Pobitzer, Austria	4
14	Vasu Duzhiy, Russia	4
15	Edward Kelley, USA	3
16	Ayojan Stojanovich, Serbia	3
17	Pushkar C. Mullauer, Switzerland	3
18	Ratin Boulton, Australia	3
19	Trishul Cherns, Canada	3
20	Galya Vladimir Balatskyy, Ukraine	3
21	Yuri Trostenyuk, Ukraine	3
22	Sopan Tsekov, Bulgaria	2
23	Pradeep Hoogakker, Netherlands	1
24	Dharbhasana Lynn, New Zealand	1
25	Istvan Sipos, Hungary	1
26	Rimas Jakelaitis, Lithuania	1
27	Hans-Jurgen Schlotter, Germany	1
28	Arpan DeAngelo, USA	1
29	Baladev Pavol Saraz, Slovakia	1
30	Kuranga M.Peel, Austria	1
31	Igor Mudryck, Ukraine	1
32	William Schel, Scotland	1
33	Nirbhasa Magee, Ireland	1

	Women	
1	Suprabha Beckjord, USA	13
2	Surasa Mairer, Austria	3
3	Nidhruvi Zimmerman, Austria	1
4	Sarah Barnett, Australia	1
5	Jayasalini Abramovskikh, Russia	1

Number of Finishes by the Country

1	Slovakia	20
2	Ukraine	20
3	USA	17
4	Austria	16
5	Finland	13
6	Czech Republic	8
7	Serbia	8
8	Australia	8
9	Great Britain	7
10	Germany	5
11	Russia	5
12	Switzerland	3
13	Canada	3
14	Bulgaria	2
15	Hungary	1
16	Lithuania	1
17	New Zealand	1
18	Netherlands	1

Other Books by Stutisheel

Eat to Run. *Holistic nutrition for the ultra marathon runner.* CreateSpace Independent Publishing Platform; 3rd edition, 2014

My First Ironman. *From dream to finish.* CreateSpace Independent Publishing Platform, 2015

Esoteric Project Management. *The development and application of inner power in management.* CreateSpace Independent Publishing Platform; first edition, 2015

Books are available in paperback and kindle format at www.Amazon.com

Footnotes

1. Sri Chinmoy, Seventy-Seven Thousand Service-Trees. Agni Press, 2002
2. Sri Chinmoy, Seventy-Seven Thousand Service-Trees., Part 27. Agni Press, 2002
3. Sri Chinmoy, Seventy-Seven Thousand Service-Trees, Part 23. Agni Press, 2001
4. Sri Chinmoy, Friendship. Agni Press, 1995
5. Sri Chinmoy, Twenty-Seven Thousand Aspiration-Plants, Part 129 (#12871). Agni Press, 1990
6. Sri Chinmoy, Silence calls me. Agni Press, 1993
7. Sri Chinmoy, Seventy-Seven Thousand Service-Trees, Part 41 (#40271). Agni Press, 2004
8. Sri Chinmoy, Seventy-Seven Thousand Service-Trees, Part 32. Agni Press, 2003
9. Sri Chinmoy, Only One Power. Agni Press, New York, 2015

Made in the USA
San Bernardino, CA
25 April 2016